# TWELVE ESSENTIAL LEADERSHIP SKILLS

*A practical booklet for managers*

by

Ken Thompson

October 2018
REVISION: 0.02

Twelve Essential Leadership Skills: A practical booklet for managers

## CONTENTS

HOW TO USE THIS BOOKLET ................................................. 3
SUMMARY INFOGRAPHIC ....................................................... 4
1. SETTING UP YOUR TEAM FOR SUCCESS ......................... 5
2. EFFECTIVE TEAM DECISION-MAKING ............................. 8
3. RUNNING PRODUCTIVE TEAM MEETINGS ................... 10
4. SAFE TEAM COMMUNICATIONS ENVIRONMENTS ...... 12
5. DEALING WITH CONFLICT ............................................... 14
6. COMMUNICATING WITH SENIOR PEOPLE ................... 16
7. PRACTICAL NEGOTIATION SKILLS ................................. 18
8. COLLABORATING BEYOND TEAM BOUNDARIES .......... 20
9. EVIDENCE-BASED DECISION-MAKING .......................... 22
10. AVOIDING UNCONSCIOUS BIAS ................................. 24
11. MAKING AND MANAGING COMMITMENTS .............. 26
12. CREATING EFFECTIVE EARLY WARNING SYSTEMS ..... 28
SKILLS SELF-ASSESSMENT TEMPLATE ................................. 30
THE SYSTEMATIC GUIDES SERIES ......................................... 31
ABOUT THE AUTHOR ............................................................ 32

Twelve Essential Leadership Skills: A practical booklet for managers

## HOW TO USE THIS BOOKLET

This collection of Twelve Essential Leadership Skills describes a set of skills which, in the authors view, are each essential competencies for a proficient manager.

Each Leadership Skill is self-contained, summarised in a couple of pages and can be used in a standalone way without reference to the other skills.

The skills are quickly and easily digestible and instantly accessible for use, as required, for example, during **group learning activities** such as business simulations or problem-solving scenarios, to enhance the opportunities for practice and experiential learning.

Each skill can apply in many situations; however as a useful simplification, to make things easy, we have categorised each of the twelve skills into one of three "primary" perspectives:

**TEAM (Skills 1-4)** – concern dealing with colleagues for whom you are directly or indirectly responsible

**PARTNERS (Skills 5-8)** – concern interaction with all other colleagues including peers, bosses, senior management, third parties, customers, suppliers and other external parties

**SELF (Skills 9-12)** – provide you with tools to help you manage your thinking, decision-making, risk and commitments

The booklet also provides a **Skills Self-Assessment Template** and **free Online App** which you can use to assess your current skill levels and set development priorities.

More detail on each of the twelve skills can be found in the relevant book in the six volume "Systematic Guides Series" which are listed in the final section of the booklet.

Twelve Essential Leadership Skills: A practical booklet for managers

**SUMMARY INFOGRAPHIC**

# Twelve Essential Leadership Skills

1. Setting up your team for success
2. Effective team decision-making
3. Running productive team meetings
4. Safe team communications environments
5. Dealing with conflict
6. Communicating with senior people
7. Practical negotiation skills
8. Collaborating beyond team boundaries
9. Evidence-based decision-making
10. Avoiding unconscious bias
11. Making and managing commitments
12. Creating effective early warning systems

**Partners**

**Team**

**Self**

Twelve Essential Leadership Skills: A practical booklet for managers

## 1. SETTING UP YOUR TEAM FOR SUCCESS

RAPPORT is a useful mnemonic for setting up a team for success. This is apt as 'Rapport' can be defined as "A close and harmonious relationship in which the groups concerned understand each other's feelings or ideas and communicate well" according to *The Oxford Dictionary*.

> **Does my team have RAPPORT?**

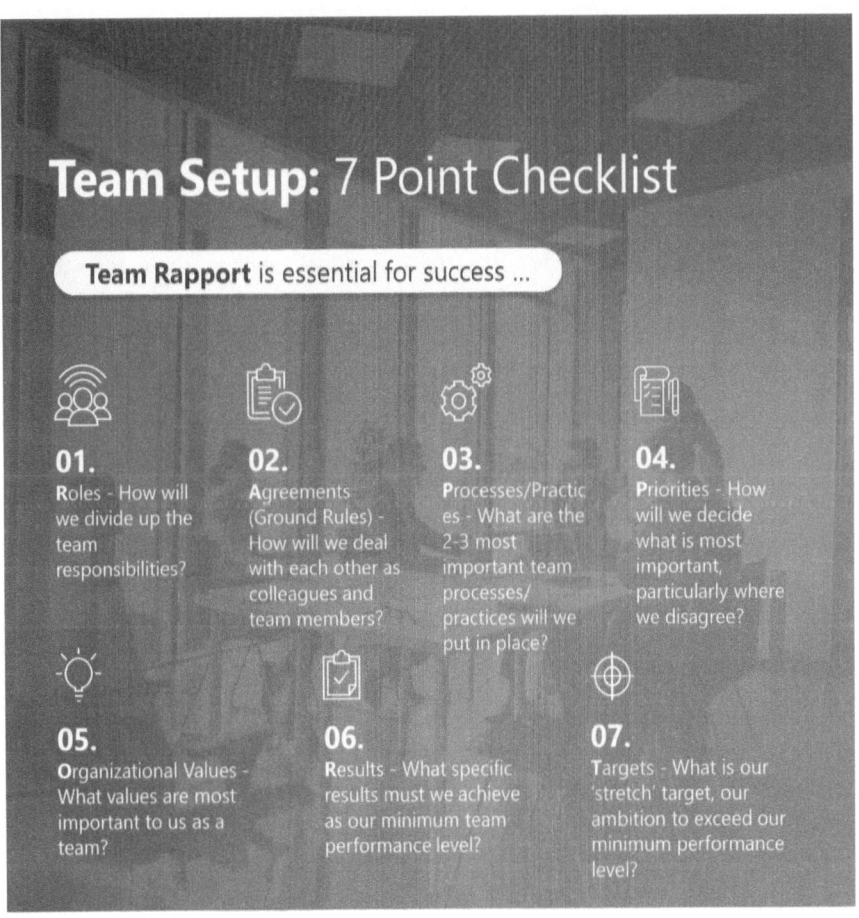

**Team Setup: 7 Point Checklist**

*Team Rapport is essential for success ...*

**01.** **R**oles - How will we divide up the team responsibilities?

**02.** **A**greements (Ground Rules) - How will we deal with each other as colleagues and team members?

**03.** **P**rocesses/Practices - What are the 2-3 most important team processes/practices will we put in place?

**04.** **P**riorities - How will we decide what is most important, particularly where we disagree?

**05.** **O**rganizational Values - What values are most important to us as a team?

**06.** **R**esults - What specific results must we achieve as our minimum team performance level?

**07.** **T**argets - What is our 'stretch' target, our ambition to exceed our minimum performance level?

# Twelve Essential Leadership Skills: A practical booklet for managers

## What Level is our Performance Management?

*In the simplest performance management model* there are just 3 levels as shown in the table below:

| | Success Conditions | Characteristics | Confidence Level |
|---|---|---|---|
| 3 | Unconditional | Professional / Resilient | Stake Your House! |
| 2 | Unless unlucky.... | Cautious / Conservative | Stake Your Job! |
| 1 | If lucky... | Naïve Optimism | Stake A Round of Drinks! |

**LEVEL 1: Naively Optimistic**

This means the team will only succeed IF it gets lucky. For example, if a sales team need 3 sales, but only have 6 prospects and their win rate is 33% then they will only succeed if they get lucky. This is very weak form of performance management as it offers no consistency.

**LEVEL 2: Cautious / Conservative**

This means that the team will succeed UNLESS they are unlucky. For example, if a sales team need 3 sales, but have 12 prospects and their win rate is 33% then they will only fail if they are unlucky. This is stronger performance management than the lower level – teams should succeed most of the time but they will still frequently fail.

**LEVEL 3: Professional / Resilient**

This means that a team has risk assessed the things which could go wrong and built resilience into their plans to reduce and mitigate the impact on their performance. Note this is not an absolute guarantee that they will always succeed – nobody can promise that. This is the level of performance which organizational teams should be aiming for as it offers a consistency of result which their leaders and colleagues can rely when they make important plans and investments!

# Twelve Essential Leadership Skills: A practical booklet for managers

> **Must anyone else lose (or win) for my team to win?**

**Is achievement of your team objectives contingent on:**

  a) Some other team ALSO achieving their objectives (Co-Dependency)

  *and/or*

  b) Some other team NOT achieving their objectives (Competition)

**In a Co-Dependency scenario,** you may also need to monitor and help the other team or teams. **In a Competition scenario,** you need to decide whether you really must be in direct competition with another team to achieve your objectives? This emphasizes the importance of goal setting which drive all team behaviours. For example, instead of the goal of having the highest sales of all teams (directly competitive) you might consider instead the goal of your sales exceeding some threshold value (indirectly-competitive)?

## 2. EFFECTIVE TEAM DECISION-MAKING

> The way a team 'decides to decide' is the most important decision it will ever make.

In the excellent book, "Why Teams Don't Work", the authors identify seven different decision-making methods for teams. If a team is planning to make a major decision, it should, wherever possible, discuss and agree on HOW the decision will be reached <u>before</u> the actual decision-making discussion starts.

At the beginning of the meeting, the team leader should introduce the decision which needs to be made and then propose and gain agreement on the decision-making method before the decision discussion begins.

### 1. Consensus

Consensus decision making is where all team members get a chance to air their opinions and must ultimately agree on the outcomes. If any team member does not agree, discussions continue. Compromise must be used so that every team member can agree with and commit to the outcomes. Can be very time-consuming.

### 2. Majority Rule

Majority decision making is democracy in action. The team votes, the majority wins.

### 3. Minority Rule

Minority decision making usually takes the form of a subcommittee of a larger team that investigates the information and makes recommendations for action.

### 4. Averaging

Averaging is the epitome of compromise. Team members haggle, bargain, cajole, and negotiate an intentional middle position. This has been more recently referred to as the "Wisdom of Crowds" and has been shown to be most effective where specialised knowledge is NOT key to the decision.

## 5. Expert

If the team doesn't already have one in the team, find or hire an expert. Listen to what the expert says and follow the expert's recommendations. This has been more recently referred to as the "Collective Intelligence" and has been shown to be most effective where specialised knowledge IS key to the decision. Obviously the key pre-decision is selecting the best expert! A variation on this is where the expert only brings a recommendation – it is still up to the team to accept it or reject it.

## 6. Authority Rule without Discussion

This is where there is no room for discussion, as with predetermined decisions handed down from higher authority. Trust is often killed with this method.

## 7. Authority Rule with Discussion

This method is also known as Participative Decision Making. Under this method, those in the decision-making role make it clear from the onset that the task of decision making is theirs. Then, they join in a lively discussion of the issues. Their opinions count just like other team members. When they have heard enough to make an educated decision, they cut off the discussion, make the decision, and then get back to all team members to let them know how their inputs affected their decision.

## 3. RUNNING PRODUCTIVE TEAM MEETINGS

> **Meetings take minutes but waste hours!**

There are basically 4 types of meeting in organizations:

- Operational Meetings – frequent, fast and short-term focus
- Strategy Meetings – future focussed, speculative, brain-storming
- Problem-Solving Meetings – adhoc, urgent and action-oriented
- Relationship Meetings – dealing with building or repairing team spirit and trust

It is important to be clear at the outset of the primary type of meeting you plan to have as you generally cannot easily keep switching between the different types all in the same meeting. For example, you might have experienced the frustration of a meeting where someone was doing blue sky thinking (strategy) which someone else was tearing to pieces because they thought it was a problem-solving meeting!

> **Decide and make clear to invitees what type of meeting you are inviting them to attend!**

Meetings tend to be shorter, more productive and less frustrating if the following roles (or equivalent) are allocated to participants <u>before</u> any meeting starts - Customer, Facilitator, Timekeeper, Scribe and Sensor.

Normally the main team leader will allocate these roles as appropriate:

### Customer

The person who, given their role, has the biggest need for the meeting to produce a successful outcome. Being the meeting customer, they decide if they are satisfied with the meeting. This is often the main team leader but not always. For example, if the meeting is addressing team member complaints then a team member might be a more appropriate customer.

# Twelve Essential Leadership Skills: A practical booklet for managers

## Facilitator

Generally steers and oils the running of the meeting and makes sure it follows any methods it agreed, for example, team decision-making. Also makes sure the customer gets what they need (sometimes in spite of the customer). Also if the meeting is being conducted using any form of virtual meeting technology they need to be able to give help and fix problems.

## Timekeeper

Ensures that the meeting always knows where it stands with respect to time so that it allocates/reallocates appropriate time to items in a sensible way. Mismanagement of time is one of the biggest meeting problems. If you have 10 decisions to make in one hour and half-way through you have only made one decision then you have a timekeeping problem. You will need to quickly re-plan the last half of the meeting.

## Scribe

Takes notes during the meeting and produces actions/notes afterwards.

## Sensor

The objective is having somebody 'sense' the temperature of the meeting and to spot unhelpful group moods. For example, resignation or complaint. The sensor should also make sure the meeting remains in the optimal mood for the type of meeting. For example, a strategy meeting may need a mood of speculation and openness whereas a problem-solving meeting may require a mood of attention to detail and challenge.

This role is sometimes also played by the Facilitator.

> **Meetings are just like teams. No roles? No results!**

## 4. SAFE TEAM COMMUNICATIONS ENVIRONMENTS

> Team Leaders who don't listen quickly create teams where no one has anything to say.

Teams need a safe environment (think **SPACE** – Safe, Positive, Authentic, Communications Environment) - where each team member feels comfortable to be able to have honest and sometimes very difficult conversations with you and other team members. To establish such environments, it is necessary for team members to be able to distinguish between what is an OPINION and what is a FACT.

### Facts are True or False - Opinions are Useful or Not Useful

A fact is something which can be verified objectively by two independent witnesses. "It rained in some parts of Belfast today" is a fact. An opinion, however, is a subjective judgement over which two independent witnesses may disagree. Based on the same fact I might voice the opinion "Northern Ireland is not a great place to live in because of the poor summers" but a local farmer might offer exactly the opposite opinion. Facts "ground" our opinions but don't make them into facts. Grounded opinions are generally more useful than ungrounded ones but neither are true or false.

It follows that whilst facts can be verifiably true or false, opinions can never be verifiably true or false; they can only be useful or not useful to the hearer.

### Why is this important for Team Communications?

Without paying close attention to these distinctions, if you try to tell me that I could have done something better or differently, then, I may listen to this as a "fact" and feel that this is a personal attack on me rather than helpful feedback. My normal reaction will also be to dispute it as a "true fact" and argue the opposite. However, if I understand it is only an opinion, which can never be true or false, I can listen to it in a non-defensive way.

Likewise, if I am giving you feedback, but casual about these distinctions, I may try and argue and prove that I am in the right and my way of seeing is the only reasonable way of looking at the situation. This can render my feedback very hard to listen to and ultimately useless to the hearer in terms of them using it to change or improve.

# Twelve Essential Leadership Skills: A practical booklet for managers

This might all just seem common sense, but unless a team practices speaking and listening using these distinctions, then there will not be a safe communications environment. This means that important things which were absolutely vital for the team's success will either be left unsaid or unheard.

> The serious team leader must become the shining example of what a safe team communications environment looks like by encouraging honest feedback and challenge of their own opinions by colleagues on both a one-to-one and a team basis.

**Do you have a safe team communications environment?**

- Do I encourage my team members to challenge me?
- Do I react in a positive way when I am challenged and how do I know this?
- Are my team members prepared to challenge each other?
- Is there evidence of my team members helping and being helped by each other?
- Do issues take a long time to be surfaced or just fester away?

## 5. DEALING WITH CONFLICT

> If you find the perfect team leave it immediately before you destroy it!

Conflict is inevitable in all teams. In fact the most effective teams have lots of conflict which they do not shy away from recognising and attempting to address. Best practice in conflict resolution generally follows an escalation process along the following lines:

### LEVEL 1

A point of conflict is identified between two team members which is damaging to the team and they cannot sort out themselves. At least one of the team members decides to flag it as an issue they need help with.

### LEVEL 2

Both parties are encouraged to make one last attempt to resolve the issue themselves, but if they cannot then go to Level 3.

### LEVEL 3

An agreed third party (e.g. another team member) tries to help the parties reach a resolution. An important skill at this stage for the third party is to be able to determine if both parties are open to being helped in 'breaking deadlock'. If you lack this skill you can waste a lot of time just going through the motions. Here are two great questions (credit to *Stephen Covey*'s 7 "Habits of Highly Effective People") which can help you determine if there is space and appetite for a negotiated solution:

> **Question 1:** Would you be prepared to search for a solution which is better than the one you have brought with you?

> **Question 2:** Are you prepared to articulate the other person's concern to their satisfaction before starting negotiation?

If you can get a YES to at least one of these questions you will have opened up a space for collaboration. If you get two NO's you are in a situation where both sides are entrenched and no longer interested in the other party's point of view. Don't waste any more time and energy - escalate to the next level!

## Twelve Essential Leadership Skills: A practical booklet for managers

**LEVEL 4**

The issue is given to another agreed third party (e.g. a team leader) to make a decision which is then binding on both parties. Your process could be as simple as this as long as you identify how third parties become involved. It is also useful to agree a timeline for each level to avoid an issue festering away and distracting the team. You should also agree to what extent other non-impacted team members are briefed (or not) on what is happening.

Twelve Essential Leadership Skills: A practical booklet for managers

## 6. COMMUNICATING WITH SENIOR PEOPLE

> As a team leader you must be effective at communicating with senior people inside and outside your organization. This may be on a one-to-one basis or meeting with a group. You may often only have a short time with senior people who can come across as impatient for you to "cut to the chase."

Before we summarize good senior communication techniques it is worth reminding ourselves that although communication involves providing *information* this is seldom the main objective, which is of course to **influence** others and usually to gain **commitment** to specific actions.

This brings us to the important topic of best practice in *engaging people for change* which is summarized nicely in the diagram below which identifies 4 distinct stages in engagement:

1. Insight and Relationship
2. Understanding and Influencing
3. Commitment
4. Support and Development

If you use this approach and don't try to skip stages you can avoid the worst problems in business communications such as seeking commitment from a person who you have an issue with or have no idea what is important to them.

# Twelve Essential Leadership Skills: A practical booklet for managers

*Nancy Duarte*, an American speaker, writer and CEO, has published an excellent article in the Harvard Business Review entitled "How to Present to Senior Executives." Nancy offers five great tips:

### Summarise up front

Assume there is a good chance that a key person may have to leave suddenly, so use the first five minutes to summarise your pitch and any "asks" you may have.

### Set expectations

Tell the group that you will be doing a short summary first, before going into the detail. This makes it less likely you will be constantly interrupted.

### Create a summary

Create a one-page executive summary with supporting slides that you can use if you get pressed to "cut to the chase" or "give me the one-minute version". You should summarise *"what the senior players need to know to make the decision you need them to make"*. You might consider the following as a useful guide:

- The Problem or Opportunity
- The impact (Why Important?)
- The Urgency (Why Now?)
- The different Action Options (including "doing nothing")
- The Costs and Benefits of each option (over an appropriate timeline)
- Your recommendation (ideally)

### Give them what they asked for

Be clear on why you were invited to meet the group and address this <u>first</u> before you address whatever else you need.

### Rehearse

Finally, before you meet them, run things through with a colleague who has senior communications experience and insist on frank feedback.

## 7. PRACTICAL NEGOTIATION SKILLS

> **You don't get what you deserve – you get what you negotiate!**

A key management skill is negotiation. You will need to negotiate with Customers, Leaders, Stakeholders, Key Influencers, Senior Users, Team members and Project Partners. One of most successful approaches to negotiation is known as principle-based or principled negotiation, made popular by the book "Getting to Yes" by *Roger Fisher* and *William Ury*. "Getting to Yes", is the definitive text on modern negotiation practices.

Principled negotiation is based around four simple principles:

### 1. Separate the people from the problem

The negotiation will go better and will be more collaborative if you can take ego and emotions out of the conversation.

### 2. Focus on interests rather than positions

The difference between a position and an interest is best illustrated by a short story. A husband and wife both want an orange but they only have one between them. If they negotiate by positions, they will split the orange in two. However, if the couple negotiate by interests, they may discover that the woman wants the orange peel to make jam and the man wants to eat the orange fruit. They can then agree a "win-win". Note: Negotiation by positions often end up in a compromise which suits neither party.

### 3. Generate options for mutual gain

If focusing on interests is all about listening to each other, then generating options for mutual gain builds on this. It encourages both parties to work together, collaborate and create "win-win" options. It is very important that this step is undertaken in a mood of speculation and brainstorming. The objective is to create lots of potential alternatives for review rather than to quickly find the best one – that comes in the next step.

### 4. Insist on using objective criteria

If you have done the previous steps well, you will have a reasonable list of "candidate solutions." Now you need to review this list in a systematic way, against a pre-agreed set of criteria, in order to find the best solution for both parties. Some critics of principled negotiation suggest that those using this approach can be easily exploited by hard-nosed negotiators on the other side who pretend to say all the right things but are just looking out for their own interests. A powerful tool within principled negotiation which can protect against "power negotiators" is the BATNA (Best Alternative to a Negotiated Agreement). A BATNA supports the principle that no deal is better than a bad deal and that you can always walk away.

For example, say you are meeting with a prospective supplier of a service that you wish to purchase. The BATNA in this case could simply be you sharing, near the beginning of the meeting, that you have already identified another supplier who can meet your requirements and costs. Before you go back to them to close the deal, you wish to see what this new supplier can offer.

## 8. COLLABORATING BEYOND TEAM BOUNDARIES

> A fundamental principle of "effective systems" is that to optimize the whole you must sub-optimize the parts. In many organizations it is the other way round – the parts (departments and teams) are optimized thus sub-optimizing the whole (business unit or enterprise).

No matter how good your team is, it is unlikely that you will be able to achieve your goals without help from somebody else. Good managers understand the importance of collaboration. However "collaboration" can take many forms and when people talk about 'collaborating' they may be all talking about something different and therefore find it difficult to reach any meaningful agreement. We have found it useful to think about 3 progressive "levels" of collaboration – each level very different from the other and summarised in the diagram below:

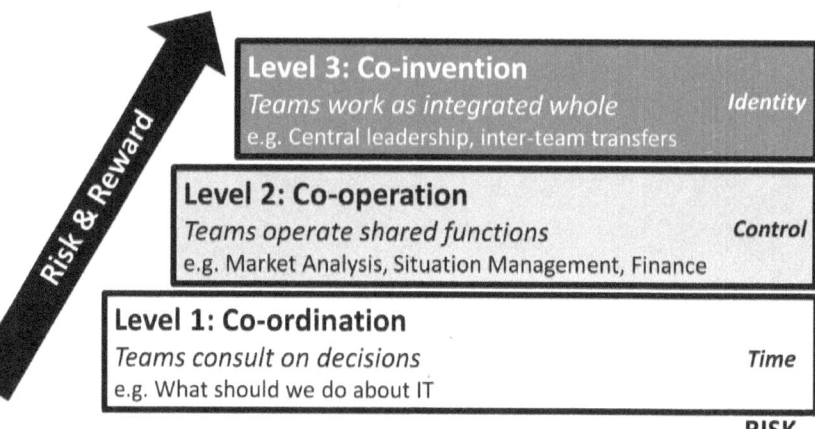

# Twelve Essential Leadership Skills: A practical booklet for managers

## LEVEL 1 - Collaboration as …. Co-ordination

At the lowest level of collaboration we have *Co-ordination* such as teams consulting on common problems. The risk is low with the biggest downside being you have wasted your time. Likewise the reward is also low.

> Where do I need to increase/improve my team's CO-ORDINATION to achieve success?

## LEVEL 2 - Collaboration as …. Co-operation

At the middle level of collaboration we have *Co-operation* such as teams agreeing to co-resource or take a joint approach to something. The risk is medium with the downside being a loss of control. Likewise the reward is also medium with efficiency savings around duplication of effort.

> Where do I need to increase/improve my team's CO-OPERATION to achieve success?

## LEVEL 3 - Collaboration as …. Co-invention

At the highest level of collaboration we have *Co-invention* such as teams agreeing to pool resources strategically under a combined leadership and decisions structure.. The risk is high with the downside being a loss of identity as you and your objectives become subsumed into and subservient to a greater whole. Likewise the reward is also high with huge efficiencies around optimizing the deployment of resources for the greater good.

> Where do I need to increase/improve my team's CO-INVENTION to achieve success?

## 9. EVIDENCE-BASED DECISION-MAKING

> "Everyone is entitled to their own opinion, but not their own facts."
>
> *Daniel Patrick Moynihan, former US Senator*

These questions are two important tools within the discipline known as "Evidence-Based" decision-making in contrast to the more popular discipline of "Gut-Feel" decision-making. Two other important tools within evidence-based decision-making are the "Five Whys" and the Knowledge Matrix.

**Who Says and So What**

"Who Says?" is about finding the original source of the news. If you cannot locate the primary source it is a pretty good sign the news may be suspect. Also when you do locate the source you may well find that it says something very different from how it has been spun!

"So What" asks the question - is the interpretation of this "fact" as meaning X, reasonable and the best among many potential interpretations.

**Five Whys (Root Cause Analysis)**

The "Five Whys" technique was invented many years ago by the Total Quality and Lean Communities to ensure that the right root problem is being solved and not just one of its symptoms.

It is described in many places on the web which you can google, and which I won't duplicate here except to offer a short summary of how to use "5 Whys" based on guidance from the UK National Health Service:

1. Write down the specific problem. Writing it down helps you formalise the problem and describe it accurately. It also helps a team focus on the same problem.
2. Use brainstorming to ask why the problem occurs then, write the answer down below.
3. If this answer doesn't identify the source of the problem, ask 'why?' again and write that answer down.
4. Loop back to step 3 until the team agrees that they have identified the problem's root cause. Again, this may take fewer or more than '5 whys?'

# Twelve Essential Leadership Skills: A practical booklet for managers

## The Knowledge Matrix

There is a simple 2x2 matrix (see overleaf) we can construct, with post-it notes on a flipchart, to represent the current state of our knowledge of any topic with 4 distinct cells for the purpose of identifying specific clarification actions:

|  | **KNOWN** | **UNKNOWN** |
|---|---|---|
| **KNOWN** | *Known knowns*<br><br>**Action:** Make sure the whole team know. Check any assumptions. | *Known Unknowns*<br><br>**Action:** Prioritise and find out. |
| **UNKNOWN** | *Unknown Knowns*<br><br>**Action:** What does someone else in your team know that you all need to know. | *Unknown Unknowns*<br><br>**Action:** Keep monitoring and be open minded for game changers. |

So for example, the cell *Unknown Knowns* (bottom left) identifies important things which one member of you team or network may know which would be very helpful if you also knew!

To find this out you need to be willing and able to engage in conversations with your network where you ask, "Is there anything else you think I need to know here?"

## 10. AVOIDING UNCONSCIOUS BIAS

> Unconscious Bias is the invisible spectacles through which we all automatically see our worlds.

Every leader views life through a filter which automatically colours their interpretation of everything they see. Taken to extreme it means you see your own interpretations as "the truth" which is very dangerous and also in a social situation such as a team can quickly turn your team members into just blindly following your orders and no longer thinking for themselves.

**Mental Models**

Mental Models are our personal mental representations of how things work. There are two types of Mental Model. Explicit Mental Models are what we say and often think we believe whereas Implicit Mental Models are what we actually believe (discovered only in taking action and often a surprise to us!)

**Golden Rules**

In the early stages of new skill acquisition we create Mental Models with conditional rules such as "IF I am standing on the baseline THEN do not volley the ball back", to use a simple example from tennis. As we become more proficient, we solidify those rules which work well and we discard or change those rules which don't work so well. An inevitable part of this process is that we unconsciously make some rules **absolute** rather than conditional.

Thus in the tennis example, our rule might become "NEVER volley the ball" or "ALWAYS volley the ball". When we de-conditionalize a rule it becomes a Golden Rule, so-called because it has delivered good results for us consistently in the past. Ironically however, Golden Rules can be THE major obstacle to us achieving our next level of performance. To unblock this we need to go back to our Mental Models and spot the Golden rules, review them and throw some away. This process is known as *Un-Learning*.

# Twelve Essential Leadership Skills: A practical booklet for managers

## The Ladder of Inference

The figure below shows how different people can travel journey from an agreed observation to vastly different conclusions, beliefs and actions.

| |
|---|
| ***Actions*** <br> **I take actions based on my beliefs** |
| ***Beliefs*** <br> I adopt beliefs about the world |
| ***Conclusions*** <br> I draw conclusions |
| ***Assumptions*** <br> I make assumptions based on the meanings |
| ***Meanings*** <br> I add meanings – cultural and personal |
| ***Data*** <br> I select specific data from my observations |
| ***Observations*** <br> I observe and experience |

It is highly effective if your "ladder" can be shared with the other party, who should also be invited to construct their own version – all starting with the same shared observation e.g.," You whispered something to your colleague at a critical point in today's meeting with our joint customer." The conversation may continue along the lines of "this observation led me to believe that you were working against our joint interests". When you hear my conclusion, you would then be able to share with me that you were only reminding your colleague that you would have to leave the meeting very promptly to pick up your daughter as the school had just sent you a text to say she had been feeling unwell.

## 11. MAKING AND MANAGING COMMITMENTS

For teams to succeed they must deliver the commitments they make to their customers and sponsors and to do this they need to rely on commitments made by others to them.

*Fred Kofman*, in a chapter entitled "Impeccable Coordination" from his excellent book "Conscious Business", offers some tips on how manage commitments (also called "promises"). Kofman suggests how to spot "weasel" commitments, purely by the language used. For example:

- Somebody needs to do something (when everybody is responsible then nobody is responsible).

- Sharon will do that (only an individual can make a commitment - nobody can commit on behalf of anyone).

- I assume that's OK with you (people have to be asked if they commit – it cannot be assumed).

- Let me see what I can do (this is no commitment whatsoever).

- I will do my best (only slightly better).

> **A useful rule when evaluating if you are happy with a commitment being offered is would you accept such a promise from your airline pilot as you go on holiday with your family?**

### Seeking Commitments

Kofman points out that there are only six clear answers when you **seek** a commitment from someone:

1. Yes, I promise
2. No, I don't commit
3. I need clarification before I can answer
4. I promise to give you an answer by this date ("commit to commit")
5. I can promise to get it done *if*, for example, you help me for two hours or do this bit of it (a conditional commitment)
6. I counter offer - I can't do x but I could do y

# Twelve Essential Leadership Skills: A practical booklet for managers

## Making Commitments

In terms of **making** solid commitments, we need to have four *clarities* at the moment we commit:

- Do I understand the request?
- Do I believe I have the necessary skills, authority, tools and resources to fulfil the request?
- Do I believe the other people I depend on will deliver? (As the buck stops with me to deliver – I cannot blame them.)
- Have I anticipated and considered foreseeable risks? (Note "foreseeable" risks – we can't predict the future!)

## Recording Commitments

Teams should maintain a *Commitment Register* simply listing for each commitment: 1) Who is committing 2) To Whom, 3) About What and 4) By When and 5) What is its current status (On target, At risk or Off-course).

> Commitments <u>not</u> recorded (and tracked) are <u>not</u> worth the paper they are <u>not</u> written on!

## 12. CREATING EFFECTIVE EARLY WARNING SYSTEMS

> There are 3 key ingredients of an Early Warning System – effective leaders have them all.

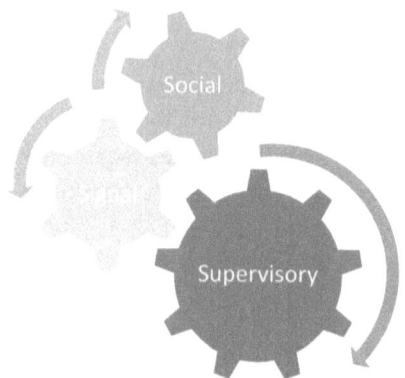

3 COMPONENTS OF AN EARLY WARNING SYSTEM

### SUPERVISORY (or FORMAL) Early Warning Systems

This is the easiest form of EWS as you get most of it automatically from good disciplines around Project Planning and Project Management. The three key characteristics of a Supervisory EWS are:

- A Project Plan with Milestone Review Points & Review Mechanisms
- Project Progress Indicators - typically resource, cost and timescales
- Project Value Indicators tracking the value the project is creating

Now you may be asking yourself is a Supervisory EWS not enough? The answer is NO - for two reasons. The first reason a Supervisory EWS is not enough is that it usually only shows "Lagging Indicators" not "Leading Indicators" of success. These two terms come from the Balanced Scorecard concept pioneered by Robert Kaplan and David Norton. Lagging indicators are great at showing value but really happen too late in the day to be used as your sole means of early warning. The second reason a Supervisory EWS is not enough is that it usually does not connect the project progress indicators with the project value indicators. For example, just because a project has used up 75% budget does not necessarily mean 75% complete in terms of its value!

# Twelve Essential Leadership Skills: A practical booklet for managers

## SIGNAL Early Warning Systems

One of the big weakness of Project Measurement Systems (like those in your Supervisory EWS) is that they tend to "make important what's measurable (easy) rather than measuring what is important (difficult)". Your Signal EWS is your "canary in the mine" where you can get a heads-up of impending problems just from the early whiff of a potential bad smell developing. The three key characteristics of a Signal EWS are:

- A Balanced Set of ...
- Predictive Leading Indicators which include ...
- Qualitative Measures or Proxies for the important intangibles

We call this EWS a "Signal" Early Warning System rather than an "Informational" EWS to stress the point that much of its value will be in non-traditional and often qualitative measures. For example, stakeholders not being available for project meetings or the level of attendance at team after-work drinks sessions in the pub.

## SOCIAL Early Warning Systems

A Social EWS is your final piece in the EWS jigsaw – the network of other people, usually outside your direct reporting line, often peers, who will look out for your "incomings". The three key characteristics of a Social EWS are:

- A Peer Network with ....
- Adequate Coverage based on ...
- Mutual Reciprocity and Trust

A Social EWS must be created one relationship/agreement at a time. It must also be constantly nurtured and usually needs to be reciprocal – "You watch my back and I will watch yours". A Social EWS also needs to cover the key aspects of the project/venture such as Stakeholder Support, End User/Customer Support, Internal Partner Support, External Partner Support and Team Support. A Social EWS is in effect your grapevine where your network partners are committed to passing on anything they hear which they judge might cause you a problem. It demands a strong level of trust as often your partners will be passing on information, sometimes shared in confidence, which can be subjective and not (yet) grounded in much supporting evidence.

Twelve Essential Leadership Skills: A practical booklet for managers

## SKILLS SELF-ASSESSMENT TEMPLATE

You can use the template below to score your current skill levels (e.g. low, medium or high competency) or to set your learning priorities:

| AREA | SKILL | SCORE/COMMENTS |
|---|---|---|
| TEAM | 1. Setting up your team for success | |
| TEAM | 2. Effective team decision-making | |
| TEAM | 3. Running productive team meetings | |
| TEAM | 4. Safe team communications environments | |
| PARTNERS | 5. Dealing with conflict | |
| PARTNERS | 6. Communicating with senior people | |
| PARTNERS | 7. Practical negotiation skills | |
| PARTNERS | 8. Collaborating beyond team boundaries | |
| SELF | 9. Evidence-based decision-making | |
| SELF | 10. Avoiding unconscious bias | |
| SELF | 11. Making and managing commitments | |
| SELF | 12. Creating effective early warning systems | |

💡 An online app version of this Leadership Skills Self-Assessment is available for your computer or mobile phone:
https://businesssimulations.com/Products/telsa

Twelve Essential Leadership Skills: A practical booklet for managers

## THE SYSTEMATIC GUIDES SERIES

The Systematic Guides Series are a collection of comprehensive, practical books each of which outlines the essential skills and practices required for a key management disciplines such as team leadership, business acumen, change management, project management or effective collaboration.

Many of the leadership factsheets in this document are summarised extracts from the relevant book:

**VOLUME 1:** A Systematic Guide to High Performing Teams (HPTs), Ken Thompson, December 2015

**VOLUME 2:** A Systematic Guide to Game-Based Learning (GBL) in Organisational Teams, Ken Thompson, January 2016

**VOLUME 3:** A Systematic Guide to Business Acumen and Leadership using Dilemmas, Ken Thompson, February 2016

**VOLUME 4:** A Systematic Guide to Change Management, Ken Thompson, July 2016

**VOLUME 5:** A Systematic Guide to Collaboration and Competition within Organisations, Ken Thompson, March 2017

**VOLUME 6:** A Systematic Guide to Project Management, Ken Thompson and Paul Hookham, July 2018

*All books are available from Amazon at cost price for training purposes.*

# Twelve Essential Leadership Skills: A practical booklet for managers

## ABOUT THE AUTHOR

Ken Thompson is an expert practitioner, author and speaker on collaboration, high performing teams, change management, game-based learning, business acumen, strategy, project management, experiential learning and social learning.

Ken's work has featured in major publications including *The Guardian Newspaper, Wired Magazine, The Huffington Post* and *The Henry Ford Magazine.*

Ken has also spoken at many international events including TEDx, the Institute for Healthcare Improvement (IHI), Learn Tech (London) and NASA.

Ken is Managing Director of BusinessSimulations.com and can be contacted via [www.businesssimulations.com/](www.businesssimulations.com/).

Twelve Essential Leadership Skills: A practical booklet for managers

www.ingramcontent.com/pod-product-compliance
Lightning Source LLC
Chambersburg PA
CBHW031559210526
45464CB00003B/1355